MIYOSHI B

READ IT! WRITE IT! RECEIVE IT!

Creating a Life of Peace and Hope

Printed in the United States of America
Copyright © 2022 The Bourget Publishing Group
All rights reserved.

Orders by U.S. trade bookstores and wholesalers.
Email us at: publisher@thebourgetgroup.net
Phone us at: 404-996-5317

The Bourget Group LLC
110 Walter Way, #856
Stockbridge, GA. 30281

First Edition
14 13 12 11 10 / 10 9 8 7 6 5 4 3 2 1

Read It! Write It! Receive It!

The Power of God's Word
About this Book

What blessings do you want to see in your life? Do you want to increase your faith, improve your health, feel more peace or joy? No matter what you are praying for, the Read It! Write It! Receive It! (RWR) series of books will help you receive the blessings you desire.

When you use RWR: Creating a Life of Peace and Hope, you are embarking on a journey of self-improvement. During this 10-week journey, you will read and reflect on scriptures that will help you focus on God's word and His promises. Reading His Word, reflecting on it, and writing about the revelations you receive, will deepen your faith in God's ability to bless you in the areas where you desire it most.

You will use these scriptures, together with prayer and systematic reflective writing, to help you activate God's Word. You will also write action steps that will help you move closer to receiving the blessings you are praying for. And at the end of your 10-week journey, you will reflect on and rejoice in the growth you have seen, and the blessings God has given you.

Trust the process, but more importantly, trust God. Your faith will move the tallest mountains and slay the biggest giants because His word says, "with God nothing will be impossible." Luke 1:37 (NKJV).

Always consult your physician or healthcare professional before stopping or changing any recommended therapeutic program. This general information is not intended to replace what your healthcare professional has prescribed. Ecclesiastes 7:12 tells us, "Here's the advantage of wisdom: It guards those who have it."

How This Book Is Organized

When you chose this book, you literally took a leap of faith! You made the decision to trust God's word and believe you will receive the blessings you desire. Read it! Write It! Receive It!: Creating a Life of Peace and Hope will help you take the steps toward obtaining these blessings.

This book is a 10-week journey. Why 10-weeks? Experts say it takes at least 66 days to develop a positive habit. By consistently using this book over the next 10 weeks, you will develop the habits of scripture reading, reflection, and prayer, which will help build and strengthen your faith. You will also write and recite affirmations, take positive action steps, and express your gratitude, all of which will set the stage for obtaining the blessings you desire.

Prior to using this book, it is recommended you familiarize yourself with it, so you understand how it is organized. Then complete the activities in the Life Assessment section. The Life Assessment activities will enable you to assess the quality of your life at the beginning of your 10-week journey. Activities include reflecting on your life and ranking your priorities, creating a Bucket List of all the activities you would like to do, and writing a vision for your life in the future.

After completing the Life Assessment section, you will work through the Weekly Action Steps sections. Each weekly section is divided into 7 Daily Action Steps. Daily Action Steps contain a Focus Scripture, reflection questions, space for affirmations and action steps, and blank pages where you can make notes and record additional thoughts.

Creating a Life of Peace and Hope is your book, so use it in the way that best meets your needs. And since the weekly sections are undated, you can complete them in any order. At the end of the 10 weeks, you will be surprised to see how much your faith has grown and how much God has blessed your life!

Life Assessment

My Life Pre-Assessment

About This Pre-Assessment

This pre-assessment will help you examine how you feel about your life. This worksheet is designed to help you identify the areas you feel you need improvement. At the end of 10 weeks, you will complete a post-assessment to see how much you have grown.

How to Use This Worksheet

Rate the eight areas of life on a scale of 1 to 10. Rate each area by coloring the numbered box that represents how you feel. Then color in all of the boxes before your rating. This will create a visual graph. Feel free to use different colored pens, pencils, markers, or crayons to create a more impactful graph.

SPIRITUALITY	1	2	3	4	5	6	7	8	9	10
RELATIONSHIPS	1	2	3	4	5	6	7	8	9	10
PHYSICAL HEALTH	1	2	3	4	5	6	7	8	9	10
EMOTIONAL HEALTH	1	2	3	4	5	6	7	8	9	10
FINANCES/MONEY	1	2	3	4	5	6	7	8	9	10
JOB/CAREER	1	2	3	4	5	6	7	8	9	10
HAPPINESS	1	2	3	4	5	6	7	8	9	10
PERSONAL GROWTH	1	2	3	4	5	6	7	8	9	10

My Prayer

What are you praying for? What blessing are you hoping to receive? Why?

....

....

....

....

....

....

....

....

....

....

....

....

....

....

....

My Bucket List

Create a bucket list of all of the things you would like to experience or achieve once you receive your blessing.

....

....

....

....

....

....

....

....

....

....

....

....

....

....

....

WHAT DO YOU NEED TO CHANGE TO MAKE YOUR LIFE BETTER?

STOP DOING	

DO LESS	

KEEP DOING	

DO MORE	

START DOING	

My Vision for My Life

Based upon how you see your life improving, write a vision for your life.

....
....
....
....
....
....
....
....
....
....
....
....
....
....
....
....

Weekly Steps of Faith

How to Use This Book

Read It! Studying God's Word

Psalm 119:18
"Open my eyes that I may see the wondrous things of your law."

God's Word contains many promises. The first step in this 10-week journey is to read His Word. Each week, you will read one Focus Scripture that is designed to help you focus on one of God's promises. As you read each Focus Scripture, you will plant the seeds of His promises in your spirit. Through this 10-week journey, you will water and grow these seeds of promise until they produce the harvest you desire.

Reflect on It! Thinking About God's Word

Psalm 119:148
"I stay awake through the night, thinking about your promise"

At the beginning of each week, you'll take a few minutes to think about the Focus Scripture and write how God's Word applies to your specific situation. You will end each day by reflecting on how you saw God move in your life. Daily reflection allows you to see and acknowledge God's work and waters your seeds of faith. And as you see Him move in your life, your faith will continue to grow.

Write It! Affirming God's Word

2 Corinthian 5:7
"For we walk by faith, not by sight."

To "walk by faith and not by sight" is to believe what you are praying for will happen, even though you don't see evidence your prayers are working. When you plant a seed in the ground, you expect the seed to sprout and eventually produce the harvest you desire. In this step, you'll plant seeds by writing Daily Affirmations.

What are Daily Affirmations?

Daily Affirmations are positive statements that affirm what you believe God is going to do. These statements are designed to help deepen your faith and trust in God and His promises.

How to Write Daily Affirmations

When you write your positive affirmations, think about what you are praying for. Then write your affirmations beginning with the words, I am or I believe. State your affirmations as if they have already happened. For example, instead of saying "I will not worry about my son", write, "I believe God is covering and blessing my son."

Here are examples of positive affirmations based upon the scripture found in **Psalm 85:8.** "I will listen to what God the Lord says; He promises peace to his people, his faithful servants—."

Examples of Daily Affirmations

- I am calm and confident about my job choice.
- I trust God. I have peace about moving out of state away from family.

Writing positive daily affirmations is one key to receiving your blessings! These affirmations represent the results you want to see in your life. You may use the Focus Scripture as the basis of your affirmations or write them based upon what you are praying for. Whatever you choose, use the same affirmations each day for at least one week. You'll also want to repeat your affirmations throughout the day to help your mind will stay focused on what you are believing God for. Your affirmations are designed to inspire you, encourage you, and motivate you to keep going, even when you feel like giving up.

Recite It! Professing the Word

Proverbs 18:21

"Death and life are in the power of the tongue, and those who love it will eat its fruit."

Each day, make it a habit to read your affirmations out loud. When you say your affirmations aloud, you are planting seeds that will produce results that reflect the words you speak. For example, if you say "I am broke", you are planting seeds of poverty. However, if you say, "I am financially stable", you are creating conditions for receiving financial stability. Reciting your affirmations out loud daily creates the conditions for bringing forth a positive harvest and increases your confidence that God will answer your prayers!

Believe It! Acting on God's Word

James 2:20
"Do you want proof...that faith without actions is worthless?"

James 2:20 says faith without actions is worthless. Many people who say they have faith just talk about having faith. For example, saying your family is at peace, while cursing out your sister, is an illustration of "worthless faith". James 2:20 says this kind of faith is worthless because it yields nothing.

In order for your faith to be effective, you must be willing to "step out in faith". When you "step out in faith", you take actions that demonstrate you believe what you are praying for will happen. These are called "Action Steps."

Each day during this journey, you will pray about the Action Steps you will take, write them down, then take those steps. At the end of the day, you can review the steps you took and reflect on how taking these steps impacted your day. The number of steps you write each day doesn't matter. What does matter is your Action Steps are specific, stated in a positive way, and are actions you are able and willing to take that day.

No matter what you are praying for, taking positive action steps to demonstrate your faith is another key to obtaining the blessings you desire.

Receive It! Receiving God's Word

Psalm 9:1
"Lord, I will give thanks to you with all my heart. I will tell about all the wonderful things you have done."

Hallelujah! Get ready for your harvest! You sowed the seeds of faith and watered them. Your seeds have taken root, sprouted, and have grown. Now, get ready for your harvest!

At the beginning of each week, you will write a prayer of praise thanking God for answering your prayer. Then, each day and at the end of each week, you will acknowledge the good things that are happening in your life. Regular expressions of gratitude to God, for even the smallest things, can help you see that God is present. These daily expressions of gratitude are proof that what you are praying for is on its way!

Another Word About Gratitude

The Lord is my strength and my shield; my heart trusts in him, and I received help. My heart rejoices, and I give thanks to him with my song.
Psalm 28:7

Expressing gratitude or giving thanks on a daily basis can be powerful and life-changing. Research studies have found that writing down what you are thankful for helps you to feel more optimistic, happier, and energetic. Studies have also found that people who write a few sentences of thanks each day are more generous toward others and suffer fewer illnesses.

Here are 3 positive effects of consistently expressing your thanks in writing on a daily basis.

1. **Expressing gratitude promotes happiness.**
Being thankful for even the smallest things helps you to become more optimistic and helps to reduce negative feelings. Giving thanks forces your mind to focus on what's good in your life, and the more you give thanks, the happier you feel.

2. **Expressing gratitude helps to improve your mental, emotional, and physical health.**
Expressing gratitude helps focus your mind on the positive aspects of your life. Expressing gratitude also allows you to focus on what you have, rather than what you don't have. This simple daily expression reduces anxiety and stress, helps to improve your immune system, and heals both the mind and body.

3. **Expressing gratitude builds your self-esteem and confidence.**
How you feel about yourself and your life on the inside affects your life on the outside. Giving thanks on a daily basis encourages you to reflect on the blessings you have in your life now. Ultimately, expressing gratitude enables you to be confident that God loves you and has "plans to prosper you and not to harm you, plans to give you hope and a future." **Jeremiah 29:11**

Notes

My Strong Tower

God is my strong tower. He providers me with a place of safety.

Focus Scripture

Believe you have received it.

"The Lord is my rock and my place of safety. He is the God who saves me. My God is my rock. I go to Him for safety. He is like a shield to me. He's the power that saves me. He's my place of safety."

Psalm 18:2 (NIRV)

Read It!: Read the focus scripture to yourself. Then read it out loud.

"The Lord is my rock and my place of safety. He is the God who saves me. My God is my rock. I go to Him for safety. He is like a shield to me. He's the power that saves me. He's my place of safety."

Psalm 18:2

Reflect on It!: What is God saying to you in this scripture?

....

....

....

....

....

....

....

....

....

Write It!: How does God strengthen you during times of trouble?

....

....

....

....

....

....

Thoughts, Reflections, and Notes

Write & Recite it!: Write your affirmations here. Then read them out loud.

....
....
....
....
....
....
....
....
....

Believe It!: List or describe the Action Steps you plan to take this week.

....
....
....
....
....

Receive It!: Write a prayer giving thanks for receiving your blessing.

....
....
....
....
....

Thoughts, Reflections, and Notes

Read It!: "The Lord is my rock and my place of safety. He is the God who saves me. My God is my rock. I go to him for safety. He is like a shield to me. He's the power that saves me. He's my place of safety."

Reflect On It!: State what you are believing God for. Why is the blessing you are praying for so important to you?

....
....
....
....

Write It!: <u>Daily Affirmations</u>
Write your affirmations in this space.
Then read them out loud.

....
....
....
....
....
....
....

Believe It!: <u>Action Steps</u>
Pray about the action steps you will take today. Then write them down.

....
....
....
....
....
....
....

Receive It!: What are you thankful for today?

....
....
....
....

Thoughts, Reflections, and Notes

Read It!: "The Lord is my rock and my place of safety. He is the God who saves me. My God is my rock. I go to him for safety. He is like a shield to me. He's the power that saves me. He's my place of safety."

Reflect On It!: State what you are believing God for. How will your life change once you receive your blessing?

....
....
....
....

Write It!: <u>Daily Affirmations</u>
Write your affirmations in this space.
Then read them out loud.

....
....
....
....
....
....
....

Believe It!: <u>Action Steps</u>
Pray about the action steps you will take today. Then write them down.

....
....
....
....
....
....
....

Receive It!: What are you thankful for today?

....
....
....
....

Thoughts, Reflections, and Notes

Read It!: "The Lord is my rock and my place of safety. He is the God who saves me. My God is my rock. I go to Him for safety. He is like a shield to me. He's the power that saves me. He's my place of safety."

Reflect On It!: State what you are believing God for. What problems will be solved once you receive your blessing?

....
....
....
....

Write It!: <u>Daily Affirmations</u>
Write your affirmations in this space.
Then read them out loud.

....
....
....
....
....
....
....

Believe It!: <u>Action Steps</u>
Pray about the action steps you will take today. Then write them down.

....
....
....
....
....
....
....

Receive It!: What are you thankful for today?

....
....
....
....

Thoughts, Reflections, and Notes

Read It!: "The Lord is my rock and my place of safety. He is the God who saves me. My God is my rock. I go to Him for safety. He is like a shield to me. He's the power that saves me. He's my place of safety."

Reflect On It!: State what you are believing God for. What is one thing you would change about yourself today in order to realize your blessing?

....
....
....
....

Write It!: <u>Daily Affirmations</u>
Write your affirmations in this space.
Then read them out loud.

....
....
....
....
....
....
....

Believe It!: <u>Action Steps</u>
Pray about the action steps you will take today. Then write them down.

....
....
....
....
....
....
....

Receive It!: What are you thankful for today?

....
....
....
....

Thoughts, Reflections, and Notes

Day 7

Reflect on it!: What went well this week?

....
....
....
....
....

Reflect on it!: What are you most thankful for?

....
....
....
....
....

Reflect on it!: What did God reveal to you this week?

....
....
....
....

Reflect on it!: What will you do differently next week?

....
....
....
....

Notes

Everlasting Father

God is my heavenly Father and He loves me.

Focus Scripture

"You are mine."

"Now this is what the Lord says. 'He created you, people of Jacob; He formed you, people of Israel. He says, "Don't be afraid, because I have saved you. I have called you by name, and you are mine.'"

Isaiah 43:1 (NCV)

Read It!: Read the focus scripture to yourself. Then read it out loud.

"Now this is what the Lord says. 'He created you, people of Jacob; He formed you, people of Israel. He says, "Don't be afraid, because I have saved you. I have called you by name, and you are mine.'"

Isaiah 43:1

Reflect on It! What is God saying to you in this scripture?

....

....

....

....

....

....

....

....

....

Write It! Is your blessing worth the effort you are making?

....

....

....

....

....

....

Thoughts, Reflections, and Notes

Write & Recite it!: Write your affirmations here. Then read them out loud.

....
....
....
....
....
....
....
....
....

Believe It!: List or describe the Action Steps you plan to take this week.

....
....
....
....

Receive It!: Write a prayer giving thanks for receiving your blessing.

....
....
....
....

Thoughts, Reflections, and Notes

Read It!: "Now this is what the Lord says. 'He created you, people of Jacob; He formed you, people of Israel. He says, "Don't be afraid, because I have saved you. I have called you by name, and you are mine."'

Reflect On It!: State what you are believing God for. What is the best decision you've made in your life?

....
....
....
....
....

Write It!: <u>Daily Affirmations</u>
Write your affirmations in this space.
Then read them out loud.

....
....
....
....
....
....
....

Believe It!: <u>Action Steps</u>
Pray about the action steps you will
take today. Then write them down.

....
....
....
....
....
....

Receive It!: What are you thankful for today?

....
....
....
....

Thoughts, Reflections, and Notes

Read It!: "Now this is what the Lord says. He created you, people of Jacob; He formed you, people of Israel. He says, "Don't be afraid, because I have saved you. I have called you by name, and you are mine.""

Reflect On It!: State what you are believing God for. What is the most valuable lesson you have learned?

....
....
....
....
....

Write It!: <u>Daily Affirmations</u>
Write your affirmations in this space.
Then read them out loud.

....
....
....
....
....
....
....

Believe It!: <u>Action Steps</u>
Pray about the action steps you will take today. Then write them down.

....
....
....
....
....
....
....

Receive It!: What are you thankful for today?

....
....
....
....

Thoughts, Reflections, and Notes

Read It!: "Now this is what the Lord says. 'He created you, people of Jacob; He formed you, people of Israel. He says, "Don't be afraid, because I have saved you. I have called you by name, and you are mine."'"

Reflect On It!: State what you are believing God for. What would you consider to be the best part of your life right now?

....
....
....
....
....

Write It!: __Daily Affirmations__
Write your affirmations in this space.
Then read them out loud.

....
....
....
....
....
....
....

Believe It!: __Action Steps__
Pray about the action steps you will take today. Then write them down.

....
....
....
....
....
....
....

Receive It!: What are you thankful for today?

....
....
....
....

Thoughts, Reflections, and Notes

Read It!: "Now this is what the Lord says. 'He created you, people of Jacob; He formed you, people of Israel. He says, "Don't be afraid, because I have saved you. I have called you by name, and you are mine."'"

Reflect On It!: State what you are believing God for. What have you done recently that makes you proud?

....
....
....
....
....

Write It!: <u>Daily Affirmations</u>

Write your affirmations in this space. Then read them out loud.

....
....
....
....
....
....
....

Believe It!: <u>Action Steps</u>

Pray about the action steps you will take today. Then write them down.

....
....
....
....
....
....
....

Receive It!: What are you thankful for today?

....
....
....
....

Thoughts, Reflections, and Notes

Day 7

Reflect on it!: What went well this week?

....
....
....
....
....
....

Reflect on it!: What are you most thankful for?

....
....
....
....
....
....

Reflect on it!: What did God reveal to you this week?

....
....
....
....
....

Reflect on it!: What will you do differently next week?

....
....
....
....

Notes

Gracious God

My God is a gracious god. He is merciful, compassionate, and caring.

Focus Scripture

God does not lie.

"God is not like people. He tells no lies. He is not like humans. He doesn't change His mind. When He says something, He does it. When He makes a promise, he keeps it."

Numbers 23:19 (NLT)

Read It!: Read the focus scripture to yourself. Then read it out loud.

"God is not like people. He tells no lies. He is not like humans. He doesn't change His mind. When He says something, He does it. When He makes a promise, He keeps it."

Numbers 23:19

Reflect on It!: What is God saying to you in this scripture?

....
....
....
....
....
....
....
....
....

Write It!: Do you need to ask forgiveness for anything you've done?

....
....
....
....
....

Thoughts, Reflections, and Notes

Write & Recite it!: Write your affirmations here. Then read them out loud.

....
....
....
....
....
....
....
....
....

Believe It!: List or describe the Action Steps you plan to take this week.

....
....
....
....

Receive It!: Write a prayer giving thanks for receiving your blessing.

....
....
....
....
....

Thoughts, Reflections, and Notes

Read It!: "God is not like people. He tells no lies. He is not like humans. He doesn't change His mind. When He says something, He does it. When He makes a promise, He keeps it."

Reflect On It!: State what you are believing God for. Is there one thing you haven't done, but would like to do?

....
....
....
....
....

Write It!: <u>Daily Affirmations</u>
Write your affirmations in this space.
Then read them out loud.

....
....
....
....
....
....
....

Believe It!: <u>Action Steps</u>
Pray about the action steps you will
take today. Then write them down.

....
....
....
....
....
....
....

Receive It!: What are you thankful for today?

....
....
....
....

Thoughts, Reflections, and Notes

Read It!: "God is not like people. He tells no lies. He is not like humans. He doesn't change His mind. When He says something, He does it. When He makes a promise, He keeps it."

Reflect On It!: State what you are believing God for. What do you need in order to do the things you want to do?

....
....
....
....
....

Write It!: <u>Daily Affirmations</u>

Write your affirmations in this space. Then read them out loud.

....
....
....
....
....
....
....

Believe It!: <u>Action Steps</u>

Pray about the action steps you will take today. Then write them down.

....
....
....
....
....
....
....

Receive It!: What are you thankful for today?

....
....
....
....

Thoughts, Reflections, and Notes

Read It!: "God is not like people. He tells no lies. He is not like humans. He doesn't change His mind. When He says something, He does it. When He makes a promise, He keeps it."

Reflect On It!: State what you are believing God for. What do you need in order to keep moving forward?

....
....
....
....
....

Write It!: <u>Daily Affirmations</u>
Write your affirmations in this space.
Then read them out loud.

....
....
....
....
....
....
....

Believe It!: <u>Action Steps</u>
Pray about the action steps you will take today. Then write them down.

....
....
....
....
....
....

Receive It!: What are you thankful for today?

....
....
....
....

Thoughts, Reflections, and Notes

Read It!: "God is not like people. He tells no lies. He is not like humans. He doesn't change His mind. When He says something, He does it. When He makes a promise, He keeps it."

Reflect On It!: State what you are believing God for. List 3 ways you can get the support you need to keep moving forward.

....
....
....
....
....

Write It!: <u>Daily Affirmations</u>

Write your affirmations in this space. Then read them out loud.

....
....
....
....
....
....
....

Believe It!: <u>Action Steps</u>

Pray about the action steps you will take today. Then write them down.

....
....
....
....
....
....

Receive It!: What are you thankful for today?

....
....
....
....

Day 7

Reflect on it!: What went well this week?

....
....
....
....
....

Reflect on it!: What are you most thankful for?

....
....
....
....
....

Reflect on it!: What did God reveal to you this week?

....
....
....
....
....

Reflect on it!: What will you do differently next week?

....
....
....
....

Notes

My Keeper

*God is my keeper. He gives me hope
and He keeps me.*

Focus Scripture

I have plans to prosper you.

"When you go through deep waters, I will be with you; When you go through rivers of difficulty, you will not drown. When you walk through the fire of oppression, you will not be burned up; the flames will not consume you. For I am the Lord, your God, the Holy One of Israel, your Savior."

Isaiah 43:2-3 (NIV)

Read It!: Read the focus scripture to yourself. Then read it out loud.

"When you go through deep waters, I will be with you; When you go through rivers of difficulty, you will not drown. When you walk through the fire of oppression, you will not be burned up; the flames will not consume you. For I am the Lord, your God, the Holy One of Israel, your Savior."
Isaiah 43:2-3

Reflect on It!: What is God saying to you in this scripture?

....
....
....
....
....
....
....
....
....

Write It!: Do you believe that God will help you? If yes, why? If no, why not?

....
....
....
....
....
....

Thoughts, Reflections, and Notes

Write & Recite it!: Write your affirmations here. Then read them out loud.

....
....
....
....
....
....
....
....
....

Believe It!: List or describe the Action Steps you plan to take this week.

....
....
....
....
....

Receive It!: Write a prayer giving thanks for receiving your blessing.

....
....
....
....
....

Day 3 *Steps of Faith* *Date*

Read It!: "When you go through deep waters, I will be with you; When you go through rivers of difficulty, you will not drown. When you walk through the fire of oppression, you will not be burned up; the flames will not consume you. For I am the Lord, your God, the Holy One of Israel, your Savior."

Reflect On It!: State what you are believing God for. Do you believe your choices help determine your life?

....
....
....
....
....

Write It!: <u>Daily Affirmations</u>
Write your affirmations in this space. Then read them out loud.

....
....
....
....
....
....
....

Believe It!: <u>Action Steps</u>
Pray about the action steps you will take today. Then write them down.

....
....
....
....
....
....
....

Receive It!: What are you thankful for today?

....
....
....
....

Thoughts, Reflections, and Notes

Read It!: "When you go through deep waters, I will be with you; When you go through rivers of difficulty, you will not drown. When you walk through the fire of oppression, you will not be burned up; the flames will not consume you. For I am the Lord, your God, the Holy One of Israel, your Savior."

Reflect On It!: State what you are believing God for. How can making different choices improve your life?

....
....
....
....
....

Write It!: <u>Daily Affirmations</u>
Write your affirmations in this space. Then read them out loud.

....
....
....
....
....
....
....

Believe It!: <u>Action Steps</u>
Pray about the action steps you will take today. Then write them down.

....
....
....
....
....
....
....

Receive It!: What are you thankful for today?

....
....
....
....

Thoughts, Reflections, and Notes

Read It!: "When you go through deep waters, I will be with you; When you go through rivers of difficulty, you will not drown. When you walk through the fire of oppression, you will not be burned up; the flames will not consume you. For I am the Lord, your God, the Holy One of Israel, your Savior."

Reflect On It!: State what you are believing God for. What choices can you make today to change your life tomorrow?

....
....
....
....
....

Write It!: __Daily Affirmations__
Write your affirmations in this space.
Then read them out loud.

....
....
....
....
....
....
....

Believe It!: __Action Steps__
Pray about the action steps you will
take today. Then write them down.

....
....
....
....
....
....

Receive It!: What are you thankful for today?

....
....
....
....

Thoughts, Reflections, and Notes

Read It!: "When you go through deep waters, I will be with you; When you go through rivers of difficulty, you will not drown. When you walk through the fire of oppression, you will not be burned up; the flames will not consume you. For I am the Lord, your God, the Holy One of Israel, your Savior."

Reflect On It!: State what you are believing God for. List 3 words to describe your life this past week.

....
....
....
....
....

Write It!: <u>Daily Affirmations</u>
Write your affirmations in this space. Then read them out loud.

....
....
....
....
....
....
....

Believe It!: <u>Action Steps</u>
Pray about the action steps you will take today. Then write them down.

....
....
....
....
....
....
....

Receive It!: What are you thankful for today?

....
....
....
....

Thoughts, Reflections, and Notes

Day 7

Reflect on it!: What went well this week?

....
....
....
....
....

Reflect on it!: What are you most thankful for?

....
....
....
....
....

Reflect on it!: What did God reveal to you this week?

....
....
....
....
....

Reflect on it!: What will you do differently next week?

....
....
....
....
....

Notes

Savior

The Lord has promised to answer when I call.

Focus Scripture

He will save me.

"The Lord says, "I will save the one who loves me. I will keep him safe, because he trusts in me. He will call out to me, and I will answer him. I will be with him in times of trouble. I will save him and honor him. I will give him a long and full life. I will save him."

Psalm 91:14-16 (NIV)

Read It!: Read the focus scripture to yourself. Then read it out loud.

"The Lord says, "I will save the one who loves me. I will keep him safe, because he trusts in me. He will call out to me, and I will answer him. I will be with him in times of trouble. I will save him and honor him. I will give him a long and full life. I will save him."

Psalm 91:14-16

Reflect on It!:   What is God saying to you in this scripture?

....
....
....
....
....
....
....
....
....
....

Write It!:   How can you apply this scripture to your life right now?

....
....
....
....
....
....

Write & Recite it!: Write your affirmations here. Then read them out loud.

....
....
....
....
....
....
....
....
....

Believe It!: List or describe the Action Steps you plan to take this week.

....
....
....
....
....

Receive It!: Write a prayer giving thanks for receiving your blessing.

....
....
....
....
....

Thoughts, Reflections, and Notes

Read It!: "The Lord says, "I will save the one who loves me. I will keep him safe, because he trusts in me. He will call out to me, and I will answer him. I will be with him in times of trouble. I will save him and honor him. I will give him a long and full life. I will save him."

Reflect On It!: State what you are believing God for. What is your greatest super power?

....
....
....
....
....

Write It!: Daily Affirmations
Write your affirmations in this space. Then read them out loud.

....
....
....
....
....
....
....

Believe It!: Action Steps
Pray about the action steps you will take today. Then write them down.

....
....
....
....
....
....
....

Receive It!: What are you thankful for today?

....
....
....
....

Thoughts, Reflections, and Notes

Read It!: "The Lord says, "I will save the one who loves me. I will keep him safe, because he trusts in me. He will call out to me, and I will answer him. I will be with him in times of trouble. I will save him and honor him. I will give him a long and full life. I will save him."

Reflect On It!: State what you are believing God for. What have you accomplished so far on this journey?

....
....
....
....
....

Write It!: <u>Daily Affirmations</u>

Write your affirmations in this space. Then read them out loud.

....
....
....
....
....
....
....

Believe It!: <u>Action Steps</u>

Pray about the action steps you will take today. Then write them down.

....
....
....
....
....
....
....

Receive It!: What are you thankful for today?

....
....
....
....

Thoughts, Reflections, and Notes

Read It!: "The Lord says, "I will save the one who loves me. I will keep him safe, because he trusts in me. He will call out to me, and I will answer him. I will be with him in times of trouble. I will save him and honor him. I will give him a long and full life. I will save him."

Reflect On It!: State what you are believing God for. What do you appreciate about your life right now?

....
....
....
....
....

Write It!: <u>Daily Affirmations</u>
Write your affirmations in this space.
Then read them out loud.

....
....
....
....
....
....
....

Believe It!: <u>Action Steps</u>
Pray about the action steps you will take today. Then write them down.

....
....
....
....
....
....
....

Receive It!: What are you thankful for today?

....
....
....
....

Thoughts, Reflections, and Notes

Read It!: "The Lord says, "I will save the one who loves me. I will keep him safe, because he trusts in me. He will call out to me, and I will answer him. I will be with him in times of trouble. I will save him and honor him. I will give him a long and full life. I will save him.""

Reflect On It!: State what you are believing God for. What can you do to appreciate your life more?

....
....
....
....
....

Write It!: <u>Daily Affirmations</u>
Write your affirmations in this space. Then read them out loud.

....
....
....
....
....
....
....

Believe It!: <u>Action Steps</u>
Pray about the action steps you will take today. Then write them down.

....
....
....
....
....
....
....

Receive It!: What are you thankful for today?

....
....
....
....

Day 7

Reflect on it!: What went well this week?

....
....
....
....
....
....

Reflect on it!: What are you most thankful for?

....
....
....
....
....
....

Reflect on it!: What did God reveal to you this week?

....
....
....
....
....

Reflect on it!: What will you do differently next week?

....
....
....
....
....

Notes

Redeemer

God keeps His promises and

redeems my life.

Focus Scripture

He lifts up the helpless.

"The Lord will keep all His promises. He is faithful in everything He does. The Lord takes good care of all those who fall. He lifts up all those who feel helpless."

Psalm 145:13-14 (NIRV)

Read It!: Read the focus scripture to yourself. Then read it out loud.

"The Lord will keep all his promises. He is faithful in everything he does. The Lord takes good care of all those who fall. He lifts up all those who feel helpless."
Psalm 145:13-14

Reflect on It!: What is God saying to you in this scripture?

....
....
....
....
....
....
....
....
....
....

Write It!: How does this scripture relate to your current condition?

....
....
....
....
....
....

Thoughts, Reflections, and Notes

Write & Recite it!: Write your affirmations here. Then read them out loud.

....
....
....
....
....
....
....
....
....

Believe It!: List or describe the Action Steps you plan to take this week.

....
....
....
....
....

Receive It!: Write a prayer giving thanks for receiving your blessing.

....
....
....
....
....

Thoughts, Reflections, and Notes

Read It!: "The Lord will keep all his promises. He is faithful in everything He does. The Lord takes good care of all those who fall. He lifts up all those who feel helpless."

Reflect On It!: State what you are believing God for. What gets you excited about living?

....
....
....
....
....

Write It!: **Daily Affirmations**
Write your affirmations in this space.
Then read them out loud.

....
....
....
....
....
....
....

Believe It!: **Action Steps**
Pray about the action steps you will take today. Then write them down.

....
....
....
....
....
....
....

Receive It!: What are you thankful for today?

....
....
....
....

Thoughts, Reflections, and Notes

Read It!: "The Lord will keep all his promises. He is faithful in everything He does. The Lord takes good care of all those who fall. He lifts up all those who feel helpless."

Reflect On It!: State what you are believing God for. What would help make you more excited about your life?

....
....
....
....
....

Write It!: <u>Daily Affirmations</u>
Write your affirmations in this space.
Then read them out loud.

....
....
....
....
....
....
....

Believe It!: <u>Action Steps</u>
Pray about the action steps you will take today. Then write them down.

....
....
....
....
....
....
....

Receive It!: What are you thankful for today?

....
....
....
....

Thoughts, Reflections, and Notes

Read It!: The Lord will keep all his promises. He is faithful in everything He does. The Lord takes good care of all those who fall. He lifts up all those who feel helpless."

Reflect On It!: State what you are believing God for. Who is/are your biggest cheerleader(s)?

....
....
....
....
....

....
....
....
....
....
....
....

Believe It!: <u>Action Steps</u>
Pray about the action steps you will take today. Then write them down.

....
....
....
....
....
....

Receive It!: What are you thankful for today?

....
....
....
....

Thoughts, Reflections, and Notes

Read It!: The Lord will keep all his promises. He is faithful in everything He does. The Lord takes good care of all those who fall. He lifts up all those who feel helpless."

Reflect On It!: State what you are believing God for. What support do you need in order to keep going?

....
....
....
....
....

Write It!: <u>Daily Affirmations</u>
Write your affirmations in this space. Then read them out loud.

....
....
....
....
....
....
....

Believe It!: <u>Action Steps</u>
Pray about the action steps you will take today. Then write them down.

....
....
....
....
....
....
....

Receive It!: What are you thankful for today?

....
....
....
....

Thoughts, Reflections, and Notes

Day 7

Reflect on it!: **What went well this week?**

....
....
....
....
....
....

Reflect on it!: **What are you most thankful for?**

....
....
....
....
....

Reflect on it!: **What did God reveal to you this week?**

....
....
....
....
....

Reflect on it!: **What will you do differently next week?**

....
....
....
....

Notes

Protector

I will not fear for God is with me.

Focus Scripture

Do not be afraid.

"I am the Lord your God. I take hold of your right hand. I say to you, 'Do not be afraid. I will help you.'... But do not be afraid."

Isaiah 41:13-14 (NIRV)

Read It!: Read the focus scripture to yourself. Then read it out loud.

"I am the Lord your God. I take hold of your right hand. I say to you, 'Do not be afraid.   I will help you'... But do not be afraid."

Isaiah 41:13-14

Reflect on It!:   What is God saying to you in this scripture?

....
....
....
....
....
....
....
....
....
....

Write It!:   How have you seen God move in your life?

....
....
....
....
....
....

Write & Recite it!: Write your affirmations here. Then read them out loud.

....
....
....
....
....
....
....
....
....

Believe It!: List or describe the Action Steps you plan to take this week.

....
....
....
....
....

Receive It!: Write a prayer giving thanks for receiving your blessing.

....
....
....
....
....

Read It!: "I am the Lord your God. I take hold of your right hand. I say to you, 'Do not be afraid. I will help you.'... But do not be afraid."

Reflect On It!: State what you are believing God for. Are you holding on to something you need to let go of?

....
....
....
....
....

Write It!: <u>Daily Affirmations</u>
Write your affirmations in this space.
Then read them out loud.

....
....
....
....
....
....
....

Believe It!: <u>Action Steps</u>
Pray about the action steps you will take today. Then write them down.

....
....
....
....
....
....
....

Receive It!: What are you thankful for today?

....
....
....
....

Thoughts, Reflections, and Notes

Read It!: "I am the Lord your God. I take hold of your right hand. I say to you, 'Do not be afraid. I will help you.'... But do not be afraid."

Reflect On It!: State what you are believing God for. Is there anyone you need to forgive?

....
....
....
....
....

Write It!: <u>Daily Affirmations</u>
Write your affirmations in this space. Then read them out loud.

....
....
....
....
....
....
....

Believe It!: <u>Action Steps</u>
Pray about the action steps you will take today. Then write them down.

....
....
....
....
....
....
....

Receive It!: What are you thankful for today?

....
....
....
....

Thoughts, Reflections, and Notes

Read It!: "I am the Lord your God. I take hold of your right hand. I say to you, 'Do not be afraid. I will help you.'.. But do not be afraid."

Reflect On It!: State what you are believing God for. What has God shown you recently?

....
....
....
....
....

Write It!: <u>Daily Affirmations</u>
Write your affirmations in this space. Then read them out loud.

....
....
....
....
....
....
....

Believe It!: <u>Action Steps</u>
Pray about the action steps you will take today. Then write them down.

....
....
....
....
....
....
....

Receive It!: What are you thankful for today?

....
....
....
....

Thoughts, Reflections, and Notes

Read It!:   "I am the Lord your God. I take hold of your right hand. I say to you, 'Do not be afraid. I will help you.'... But do not be afraid."

Reflect On It!: State what you are believing God for. What are you prepared to do to realize your dream?

....
....
....
....
....

Write It!: <u>Daily Affirmations</u>
Write your affirmations in this space.
Then read them out loud.

....
....
....
....
....
....
....

Believe It!: <u>Action Steps</u>
Pray about the action steps you will
take today. Then write them down.

....
....
....
....
....
....
....

Receive It!:   What are you thankful for today?

....
....
....
....

Thoughts, Reflections, and Notes

Day 7

Reflect on it!: What went well this week?

....
....
....
....
....
....

Reflect on it!: What are you most thankful for?

....
....
....
....
....
....

Reflect on it!: What did God reveal to you this week?

....
....
....
....
....

Reflect on it!: What will you do differently next week?

....
....
....
....
....

Notes

Shepherd

The Lord is my shepherd.

He takes care of my needs.

Focus Scripture

Trust Him.

"Trust in the Lord and do good. Then you will live safely in the land and prosper. Take delight in the Lord, and He will give you your heart's desires. Commit everything you do to the Lord. Trust Him, and He will help you."

Psalm 37:3-4 (NIV)

Read It!: Read the focus scripture to yourself. Then read it out loud.

"Trust in the Lord and do good. Then you will live safely in the land and prosper. Take delight in the Lord, and He will give you your heart's desires. Commit everything you do to the Lord. Trust Him, and He will help you."

Psalm 37:3-4

Reflect on It!: What is God saying to you in this scripture?

....
....
....
....
....
....
....
....
....

Write It!: What makes up the foundation upon which you've built your life?

....
....
....
....
....
....

Write & Recite it!: Write your affirmations here. Then read them out loud.

....
....
....
....
....
....
....
....
....

Believe It!: List or describe the Action Steps you plan to take this week.

....
....
....
....

Receive It!: Write a prayer giving thanks for receiving your blessing.

....
....
....
....
....

Read It!: "Trust in the Lord and do good. Then you will live safely in the land and prosper. Take delight in the Lord, and He will give you your heart's desires. Commit everything you do to the Lord. Trust Him, and He will help you."

Reflect On It!: State what you are believing God for. If you could relive yesterday, what would you do differently?

....
....
....
....
....

Write It!: <u>Daily Affirmations</u>
Write your affirmations in this space.
Then read them out loud.

....
....
....
....
....
....

Believe It!: <u>Action Steps</u>
Pray about the action steps you will
take today. Then write them down.

....
....
....
....
....
....

Receive It!: What are you thankful for today?

....
....
....
....

Read It!: "Trust in the Lord and do good. Then you will live safely in the land and prosper. Take delight in the Lord, and He will give you your heart's desires. Commit everything you do to the Lord. Trust Him, and He will help you."

Reflect On It!: State what you are believing God for. What is the biggest change you've seen so far?

....
....
....
....
....

Write It!: <u>Daily Affirmations</u>
Write your affirmations in this space.
Then read them out loud.

....
....
....
....
....
....
....

Believe It!: <u>Action Steps</u>
Pray about the action steps you will
take today. Then write them down.

....
....
....
....
....
....

Receive It!: What are you thankful for today?

....
....
....
....

Thoughts, Reflections, and Notes

Read It!: "Trust in the Lord and do good. Then you will live safely in the land and prosper. Take delight in the Lord, and He will give you your heart's desires. Commit everything you do to the Lord. Trust Him, and He will help you."

Reflect On It!: State what you are believing God for. Are you doing anything to sabotage your progress?

....
....
....
....
....

Write It!: <u>Daily Affirmations</u>
Write your affirmations in this space. Then read them out loud.

....
....
....
....
....
....
....

Believe It!: <u>Action Steps</u>
Pray about the action steps you will take today. Then write them down.

....
....
....
....
....
....
....

Receive It!: What are you thankful for today?

....
....
....
....

Thoughts, Reflections, and Notes

Read It!: "Trust in the Lord and do good. Then you will live safely in the land and prosper. Take delight in the Lord, and He will give you your heart's desires. Commit everything you do to the Lord. Trust Him, and He will help you."

Reflect On It!: State what you are believing God for. What would you do if you knew you couldn't fail?

....

....

....

....

....

Write It!: <u>Daily Affirmations</u>
Write your affirmations in this space. Then read them out loud.

....

....

....

....

....

....

Believe It!: <u>Action Steps</u>
Pray about the action steps you will take today. Then write them down.

....

....

....

....

....

....

Receive It!: What are you thankful for today?

....

....

....

....

Thoughts, Reflections, and Notes

Day 7

Reflect on it!: **What went well this week?**

....
....
....
....
....
....

Reflect on it!: **What are you most thankful for?**

....
....
....
....
....
....

Reflect on it!: **What did God reveal to you this week?**

....
....
....
....
....

Reflect on it!: **What will you do differently next week?**

....
....
....
....
....

Notes

Faithful and True

God is faithful and true. He knows the plans He has for me.

Focus Scripture

His word produce results.

"My thoughts are not like your thoughts. And your ways are not like my ways," announces the Lord. "The heavens are higher than the earth. And my ways are higher than your ways...The words I speak are like that. They will not return to me without producing results. They will accomplish what I want them to. They will do exactly what I sent them to do."

Isaiah 55:8-9,11 (NLT)

Read It!: Read the focus scripture to yourself. Then read it out loud.

"My thoughts are not like your thoughts. And your ways are not like my ways," announces the Lord. "The heavens are higher than the earth. And my ways are higher than your ways...The words I speak are like that. They will not return to me without producing results. They will accomplish what I want them to. They will do exactly what I sent them to do."   Isaiah 55:8-9,11

Reflect on It!: What is God saying to you in this scripture?

....
....
....
....
....
....
....
....
....
....

Write It!: Write in this space what you are believing God will do in your life.

....
....
....
....
....
....

Thoughts, Reflections, and Notes

Write & Recite it!: Write your affirmations here. Then read them out loud.

....
....
....
....
....
....
....
....
....

Believe It!: List or describe the Action Steps you plan to take this week.

....
....
....
....
....

Receive It!: Write a prayer giving thanks for receiving your blessing.

....
....
....
....

Thoughts, Reflections, and Notes

Read It!: "My thoughts are not like your thoughts. And your ways are not like my ways," announces the Lord. "The heavens are higher than the earth. And my ways are higher than your ways...The words I speak are like that. They will not return to me without producing results. They will accomplish what I want them to. They will do exactly what I sent them to do."

Reflect On It!: State what you are believing God for. What do you want more of in your life?

....

....

....

....

....

Write It!: <u>Daily Affirmations</u>
Write your affirmations in this space.
Then read them out loud.

....

....

....

....

....

....

....

Believe It!: <u>Action Steps</u>
Pray about the action steps you will
take today. Then write them down.

....

....

....

....

....

....

....

Receive It!: What are you thankful for today?

....

....

....

....

Thoughts, Reflections, and Notes

Read It!: "My thoughts are not like your thoughts. And your ways are not like my ways," announces the Lord. "The heavens are higher than the earth. And my ways are higher than your ways...The words I speak are like that. They will not return to me without producing results. They will accomplish what I want them to. They will do exactly what I sent them to do."

Reflect On It!: State what you are believing God for. What do you want less of in your life?

....
....
....
....
....

Write It!: <u>Daily Affirmations</u>
Write your affirmations in this space.
Then read them out loud.

....
....
....
....
....
....
....

Believe It!: <u>Action Steps</u>
Pray about the action steps you will take today. Then write them down.

....
....
....
....
....
....
....

Receive It!: What are you thankful for today?

....
....
....
....

Thoughts, Reflections, and Notes

Read It!: "My thoughts are not like your thoughts. And your ways are not like my ways," announces the Lord. "The heavens are higher than the earth. And my ways are higher than your ways...The words I speak are like that. They will not return to me without producing results. They will accomplish what I want them to. They will do exactly what I sent them to do."

Reflect On It!: State what you are believing God for. Is there anything preventing you from moving forward?

....
....
....
....
....

Write It!: <u>Daily Affirmations</u>
Write your affirmations in this space. Then read them out loud.

....
....
....
....
....
....
....

Believe It!: <u>Action Steps</u>
Pray about the action steps you will take today. Then write them down.

....
....
....
....
....
....
....

Receive It!: What are you thankful for today?

....
....
....
....

Thoughts, Reflections, and Notes

Read It!: "My thoughts are not like your thoughts. And your ways are not like my ways," announces the Lord. "The heavens are higher than the earth. And my ways are higher than your ways...The words I speak are like that. They will not return to me without producing results. They will accomplish what I want them to. They will do exactly what I sent them to do."

Reflect On It!: State what you are believing God for. What is motivating you to keep going?

....
....
....
....
....

Write It!: <u>Daily Affirmations</u>
Write your affirmations in this space.
Then read them out loud.

....
....
....
....
....
....
....

Believe It!: <u>Action Steps</u>
Pray about the action steps you will take today. Then write them down.

....
....
....
....
....
....
....

Receive It!: What are you thankful for today?

....
....
....
....

Thoughts, Reflections, and Notes

Day 7

Reflect on it!: What went well this week?

....
....
....
....
....
....

Reflect on it!: What are you most thankful for?

....
....
....
....
....

Reflect on it!: What did God reveal to you this week?

....
....
....
....
....

Reflect on it!: What will you do differently next week?

....
....
....
....

Notes

King of Glory

He is the King of Glory,

changeless and true.

Focus Scripture

I will praise You, my God.

O Lord, You are my God. I will praise You.
I will give thanks to Your name. For You have
been faithful to do great things, plans that
You made long ago."

Isaiah 25:1 (NLV)

Read It!: Read the focus scripture to yourself. Then read it out loud.

O Lord, You are my God. I will praise You. I will give thanks to Your name. For You have been faithful to do great things, plans that You made long ago."
Isaiah 25:1

Reflect on It!: What is God saying to you in this scripture?

....
....
....
....
....
....
....
....
....
....

Write It!: Describe how God's promise makes you feel?

....
....
....
....
....
....

Thoughts, Reflections, and Notes

Write & Recite it!: Write your affirmations here. Then read them out loud.

....
....
....
....
....
....
....
....
....

Believe It!: List or describe the Action Steps you plan to take this week.

....
....
....
....

Receive It!: Write a prayer giving thanks for receiving your blessing.

....
....
....
....

Thoughts, Reflections, and Notes

Day 3   Steps of Faith   Date

Read It!: "O Lord, You are my God. I will praise You. I will give thanks to Your name. For You have been faithful to do great things, plans that You made long ago."

Reflect On It!: State what you are believing God for. What are you looking forward to?

....
....
....
....
....

Write It!: Daily Affirmations
Write your affirmations in this space. Then read them out loud.

....
....
....
....
....
....
....

Believe It!: Action Steps
Pray about the action steps you will take today. Then write them down.

....
....
....
....
....
....
....

Receive It!: What are you thankful for today?

....
....
....
....

Read It!: O Lord, You are my God. I will praise You. I will give thanks to Your name. For You have been faithful to do great things, plans that You made long ago."

Reflect On It!: State what you are believing God for. What will you keep doing?

....
....
....
....
....

Write It!: <u>Daily Affirmations</u>
Write your affirmations in this space.
Then read them out loud.

....
....
....
....
....
....
....

Believe It!: <u>Action Steps</u>
Pray about the action steps you will take today. Then write them down.

....
....
....
....
....
....
....

Receive It!: What are you thankful for today?

....
....
....
....

Thoughts, Reflections, and Notes

Read It!: O Lord, You are my God. I will praise You. I will give thanks to Your name. For You have been faithful to do great things, plans that You made long ago."

Reflect On It!: State what you are believing God for. What will you stop doing?

....
....
....
....
....

Write It!: <u>Daily Affirmations</u>
Write your affirmations in this space. Then read them out loud.

....
....
....
....
....
....
....

Believe It!: <u>Action Steps</u>
Pray about the action steps you will take today. Then write them down.

....
....
....
....
....
....
....

Receive It!: What are you thankful for today?

....
....
....
....

Thoughts, Reflections, and Notes

Read It!: O Lord, You are my God. I will praise You. I will give thanks to Your name. For You have been faithful to do great things, plans that You made long ago."

Reflect On It!: State what you are believing God for. What is the next big step you need to take?

....
....
....
....
....

Write It!: <u>Daily Affirmations</u>

Write your affirmations in this space.
Then read them out loud.

....
....
....
....
....
....
....

Believe It!: <u>Action Steps</u>

Pray about the action steps you will
take today. Then write them down.

....
....
....
....
....
....
....

Receive It!: What are you thankful for today?

....
....
....
....

Thoughts, Reflections, and Notes

Day 7

Reflect on it!: What went well this week?

....

....

....

....

....

....

Reflect on it!: What are you most thankful for?

....

....

....

....

....

....

Reflect on it!: What did God reveal to you this week?

....

....

....

....

....

Reflect on it!: What will you do differently next week?

....

....

....

....

....

Notes

Reflections

10-Week Healing Scriptures

1. "The Lord is my rock and my place of safety. He is the God who saves me. My God is my rock. I go to him for safety. He is like a shield to me. He's the power that saves me. He's my place of safety." **Psalm 18:2 (NIRV)**

2. "Now this is what the Lord says. He created you, people of Jacob; He formed you, people of Israel. He says, "Don't be afraid, because I have saved you. I have called you by name, and you are mine." **Isaiah 43:1 (NCV)**

3. "God is not like people. He tells no lies. He is not like humans. He doesn't change his mind. When he says something, he does it. When he makes a promise, He keeps it." **Numbers 23:19 (NLT)**

4. "When you go through deep waters, I will be with you; When you go through rivers of difficulty, you will not drown. When you walk through the fire of oppression, you will not be burned up; the flames will not consume you. For I am the Lord, your God, the Holy One of Israel, your Savior." **Isaiah 43:2-3 (NIV)**

5. "The Lord says, "I will save the one who loves me. I will keep him safe, because he trusts in me. He will call out to me, and I will answer him. I will be with him in times of trouble. I will save him and honor him. I will give him a long and full life. I will save him." **Psalm 91:14-16 (NIV)**

6. "The Lord will keep all his promises. He is faithful in everything he does. The Lord takes good care of all those who fall. He lifts up all those who feel helpless." **Psalm 145:13-14 (NIRV)**

7. "I am the Lord your God. I take hold of your right hand. I say to you, 'Do not be afraid. I will help you.'.. But do not be afraid." **Isaiah 41:13-14 (NIRV)**

8. "Trust in the Lord and do good. Then you will live safely in the land and prosper. Take delight in the Lord, and he will give you your heart's desires. Commit everything you do to the Lord. Trust him, and he will help you." **Psalm 37:3-4 (NIV)**

9. "My thoughts are not like your thoughts. And your ways are not like my ways," announces the Lord. "The heavens are higher than the earth. And my ways are higher than your ways. My thoughts are higher than your thoughts...The words I speak are like that. They will not return to me without producing results. They will accomplish what I want them to. They will do exactly what I sent them to do." **Isaiah 55:8-9,11 (NLT)**

10. "O Lord, You are my God. I will praise You. I will give thanks to Your name. For You have been faithful to do great things, plans that You made long ago." **Isaiah 25:1 (NLV)**

10-Week Reflections

What changes have you seen in the last 10-weeks?

....
....
....
....
....
....
....
....
....
....
....
....
....
....
....
....

Reflect on it!: How have you grown during the past 10-weeks?

....
....
....
....
....
....
....
....
....

Blessings

Date:

What Are You Grateful For?

My Life Post-Assessment

About This Post-Assessment

This post-assessment will help you gauge how you feel about your life after 10 weeks and identify areas of growth.

Rate the eight areas of life on a scale of 1 to 10. Rate each area by coloring the numbered box that represents how you feel. Then color in all of the boxes before your rating. This will create a visual graph. Feel free to use different colored pens, pencils, markers, or crayons to create a more impactful graph.

SPIRITUALITY	1	2	3	4	5	6	7	8	9	10
RELATIONSHIPS	1	2	3	4	5	6	7	8	9	10
PHYSICAL HEALTH	1	2	3	4	5	6	7	8	9	10
EMOTIONAL HEALTH	1	2	3	4	5	6	7	8	9	10
FINANCES/MONEY	1	2	3	4	5	6	7	8	9	10
JOB/CAREER	1	2	3	4	5	6	7	8	9	10
HAPPINESS	1	2	3	4	5	6	7	8	9	10
PERSONAL GROWTH	1	2	3	4	5	6	7	8	9	10

Thoughts, Reflections, and Notes

Get FREE GOODIES to support your journey!
E-mail us at:
publisher@thebourgetpublishinggroup.com
Write "PEACE Freebies" in the subject line
or
scan the image below.

SCAN FOR FREE PEACE GOODIES!

Made in the USA
Columbia, SC
27 January 2023

10343152R00102